Introduction – Big Ideas

Before reading the book, The Corn Chief, answer the following questions as a class.

Brainstorm possible answers to these questions:

I0800701

Who is a chief? Who is allowed to be a chief?
What is the role of a chief?
Why is a chief important to his/her/their community?
To be helpful and effective as a chief, what are some qualities that make the chief a good leader?
Have chiefs, traditionally, been men or women?

Activity 1 – Chief Concept Map

In the boxes below, write down qualities you think would make an excellent leader and/or chief. Then draw a symbol to represent that quality. For example, one word could be courage and you could draw a person on a mountain top.

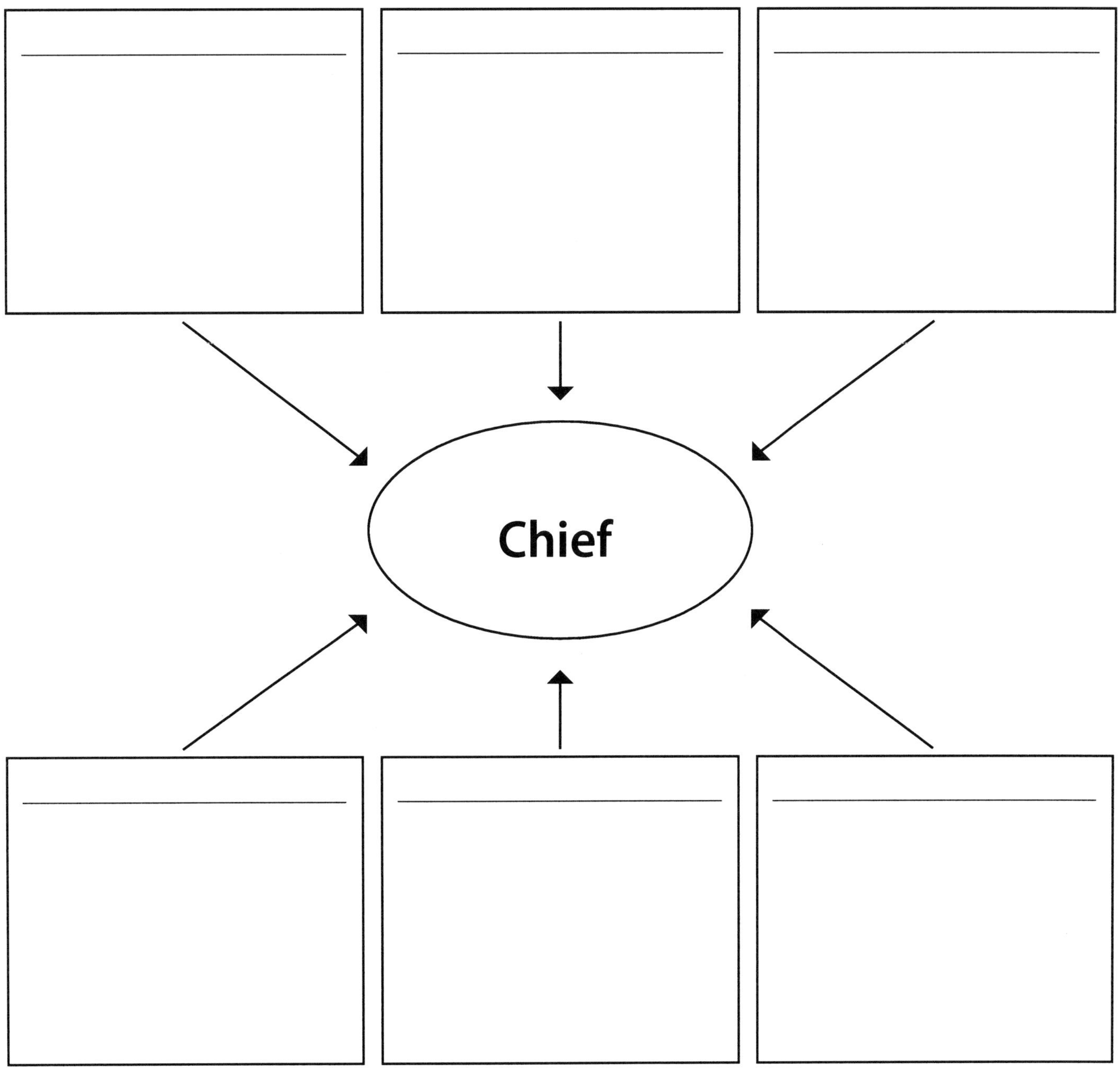

Activity 2– Rhyming Words

Fill in the blanks using the rhyming words from the story:

Page 1

A wizened chief was getting old and soon would need a ________________.

He took some seeds that would not grow and used them for a ____________.

"I've been in charge through many moons,

Now my time is ____________________."

"I must choose someone new to begin their chieftain ______________________."

He poured corn seeds into his hand and passed them out to ____________.

"I'll choose the one who grows the most, by harvest in the ______________.

Page 5

In the morning, Linny ran out to the garden and ____________________,

The corn had not started to grow atop the seeded ___________________.

She looked into her neighbour's yard and saw a little sprout.

She ran inside and found her mom to soothe her thoughts of ______________.

"I can't even get corn to grow. How can I be a ___________________?

Page 9

Three days later, Linny went out to the garden and _________________,

The replaced corn had not grown atop the seeded ___________________.

She looked into her neighbour's yard, and saw his growing _____________,

Her heart filled with disappointment, her mouth needed to _____________.

Linny went to her auntie's house, to soothe her thoughts of _____________.

"I cannot get my corn to grow, I want to be a ________________.

Activity 2 – Continued

Page 15

"Did you say "thank you" to the earth with tobacco and ___________.

Linny looked up with hopeful eyes,

"That must be what went _________________.

Page 19

As she entered the feasting hall, the room began to ________________.

Everyone else had brought some corn.

Her cheeks began to ________________.

Page 21

"Beans and squash?" the chief asked Linny.

"Why have you brought me ______________?"

Linny's lip began to quiver.

A

tear

dropped

to

her

___________ .

Page 23

So I went to see my auntie and I learned of sisters _______________.

I planted them in my garden but still no corn, you ___________!

Page 27

"Linny grew hope when she planted; persisted and grew _____________.

Grew knowledge of our traditions. She grew the most ______________.

"Leadership is more than just completion of a ______________.

It's learning that we all need help and knowing when to _____________.

Activity 3– History of the Corn Husk Doll

Corn Husk Dolls are important symbols with important cultural teachings. The following is the write up from *The Corn Chief* about the importance of Corn Husk Dolls.

Read the following as a class.

"Respectfully called the sustainers of life are the Three Sisters — Corn, Beans, and Squash. The corn husk doll is made from the husks of the most sacred crop, corn. Corn husk dolls have likely been made since the beginnings of corn agriculture more than one thousand years ago. Corn dolls protect the home, livestock, and personal wellness of the maker and their family. The corn doll may be seen as a home for the spirit of the crop.

To make the doll, the dried husks are placed in water to make them soft, then twisted and shaped to create a doll's body. Once finished, they are once again dried and turn sturdy enough to make the completed corn doll. Sometimes clothing or other pieces are also created for the doll. Traditional corn husk dolls do not have a face.

The corn husk doll came to the people of the corn. They had the most beautiful face, happy and gentle. They were tasked with watching over the children and keeping them entertained. The children loved how beautiful the doll was, and over time the corn husk doll also became aware of their beauty. They would no longer play for fear of getting dirty. They would stare at their reflection instead of looking into the faces of the children. An owl was sent to remove the face from the corn husk doll, so they would never let their vanity get in the way of their purpose in the community. To this day, the corn husk doll remains faceless."

In the box below, draw and then colour a Corn Husk Doll that comes to your mind. Remember, they should be faceless.

Activity 3 - Continued

Using the details found on the writeup on the previous page, have students make a list of important details they have learned about corn husk dolls.

Detail 1:

Detail 2:

Detail 3:

Detail 4:

The most important detail I learned about corn husks dolls is ...

Activity 4 – Personal Response

Linny went to her family members to seek advice about growing corn. Her Family shared these words with her, what does each statement mean?

"Did you plant beans and squash with it? Together they are grown."

"Each one supports the other two, grow them and you will see."

"Did you say, 'thank you' to the earth with tobacco and song?"

Have you tried growing a plant, but it didn't want to grow? What was your solution to growing the plant? Did you give up or did you continue?

What did Linny do? What do you think it means when the story says, "she dug until her fingers throbbed?"

Activity 5 – Knowledge and Growth

Linny showed determination to grow her corn to become the next chief. She never gave up even when she couldn't grow corn. When she first planted it, it didn't work so she found different ways/sources to make it grow by seeking the knowledge of others and growing through the process.

What do you think "seeking knowledge of others "means?

____

____

____

Using The *Corn Chief* as a guide, write the knowledge that was shared by each of the family members in the story.

Source	Knowledge Shared
Mom (First person in the story) ____________________ ____________________ ____________________	____________________ ____________________ ____________________
Auntie (Second person in the story) ____________________ ____________________ ____________________	____________________ ____________________ ____________________
Papa (Third person in the story) ____________________ ____________________ ____________________	____________________ ____________________ ____________________

Activity 5 – Continued

In your own life, describe a situation where you felt stuck in learning something, and you looked to others to help you with your knowledge. What was the situation?

What did you learn?

How did you feel?

Draw a picture of what you learned.

Activity 6 – Being a Leader

Discuss these questions as a whole group or in a talking circle once the book has been read.

What qualities did the chief see in Linny?

Why did he choose her?

Do you feel he made the right choice? Explain.

What skills/qualities does a chief/leader need to possess?

Draw Linny as Chief

Think about a leader in the world that you admire. It could be someone in your community, someone famous and/or someone in your school. What makes them a great leader?

____

____

____

Activity 6 – The Medicine Wheel and Leadership

Linny demonstrated many leadership skills or traits in *The Corn Chief*. These skills or traits can be summarized into four quadrants: physical, mental, emotional, and spiritual. The Medicine Wheel also has four quadrants which represent these four areas.

Utilizing the Medicine Wheel diagram, insert the different words below into the appropriate area. For example, emotional = crying, or having lots of feeling when Linny was asked by the Chief about only bringing beans and squash.

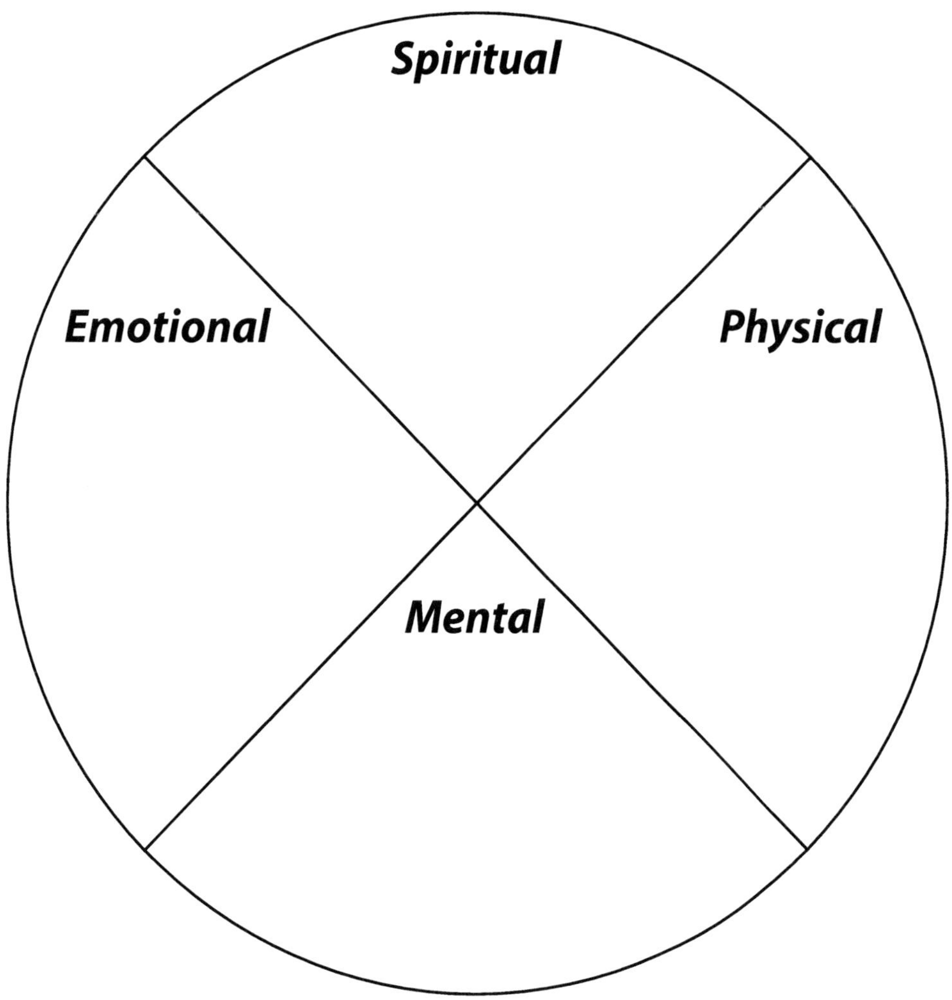

disappointment	doubtful	tilled the soil	persistent
dread	learning	planting	hopeful
traditions	I can be chief	singing	thankful
dancing	hope	love	offering tobacco

After completing the activity, circle the words that you feel make a strong, powerful and effective leader.

Activity 7 – The Medicine Wheel and Leadership

Complete the following sentences

A balanced leader thinks

____

____

____

____

A balanced leader feels

____

____

____

____

A balanced leader does

____

____

____

____

A balanced leader lives their life in a

____________________________________ way.

Activity 8 – Wordsearch

W O N T O B A C C O W D R U M P E A
H P T D I S A P P O I N T M E N T T
E E A R T H H W X R A P A P A G C I
L W M O M K R V W B P K Q T Z A C L
P B C I H A R V E S T L X D X R H L
C K N O W L E D G E M Y A T X D I E
J E T O R T R A D I T I O N S E E D
Y S P C T N X B E A N S X L T N F Z
N E I G H B O U R K A U N T I E M H
S E C O M P L E T I O N W T C V D G
K D P G I R F S Q U A S H L A J F C
X K I J P E D G R O W T H V Q L O X

AUNTIE
BEANS
CHIEF
COMPLETION
CORN
DISAPPOINTMENT
DRUM
EARTH
GARDEN
GROWTH
HARVEST
HELP
KNOWLEDGE
MOM
NEIGHBOUR
PAPA
PLANTED
SEED
SQUASH
TILLED
TOBACCO
TRADITIONS

Activity 9 – Crossword Puzzle

Down:

1. The chief said Linny grew knowledge of our________ when she grew the most inside.
2. Linny was chosen to be chief because she knew to ask for this.
3. Who gave Linny the corn to plant?
8. Who grew more corn than Linny?
9. Linny possessed this skill that a chief should have.

Across:

4. "I'll choose the one who grows the most by________ in the fall."
5. She dug the earth, planted the corn, and then she hoped and _______.
6. What traditional plant did Linny offer with her thank you song?
7. What did Linny try to grow?
10. Where did Linny plant her corn?
11. Besides beans, what else should you grow?
12. What instrument did Linny's papa play when he taught her to sing?

Activity 9 – Crossword Answer Key

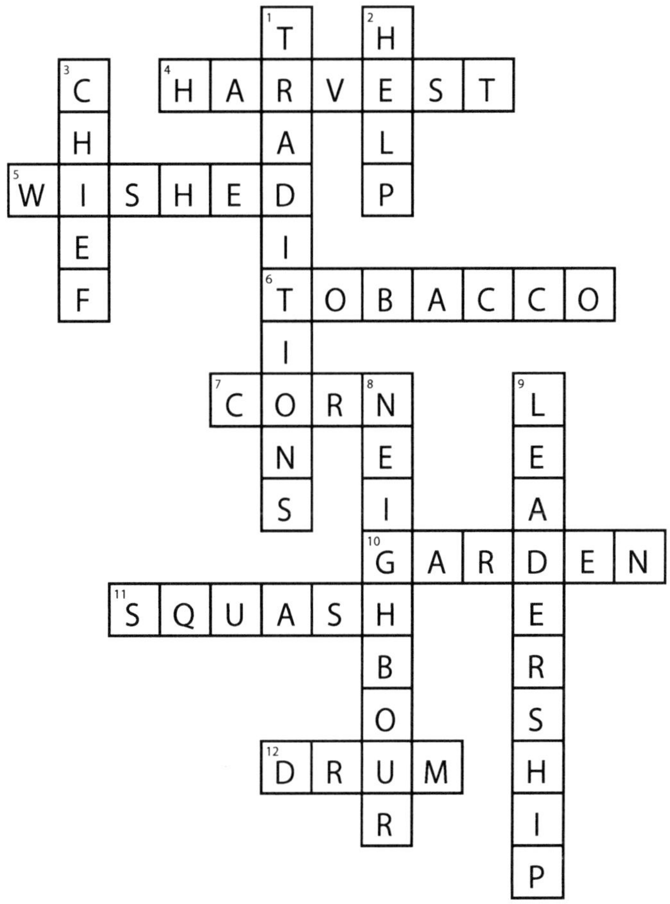

Down:

1. The chief said Linny grew knowledge of our________ when she grew the most inside.
2. Linny was chosen to be chief because she knew to ask for this.
3. Who gave Linny the corn to plant?
8. Who grew more corn than Linny?
9. Linny possessed this skill that a chief should have.

Across:

4. "I'll choose the one who grows the most by________ in the fall."
5. She dug the earth, planted the corn, and then she hoped and ________.
6. What traditional plant did Linny offer with her thank you song?
7. What did Linny try to grow?
10. Where did Linny plant her corn?
11. Besides beans, what else should you grow?
12. What instrument did Linny's papa play when he taught her to sing?